The
Chain Bridge
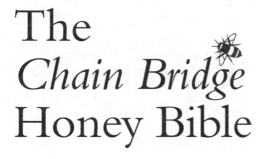
Honey Bible

Liz Ashworth

Illustrated by Bob Dewar

BIRLINN

First published in 2016 by
Birlinn Limited
West Newington House
10 Newington Road
Edinburgh
EH9 1QS

www.birlinn.co.uk

ISBN: 978 1 78027 344 0

British Library Cataloguing-in-Publication Data
A catalogue record for this book is available
from the British Library

Designed and typeset by Mark Blackadder

Printed and bound by Bell & Bain Ltd, Glasgow

Contents

Baking

Scones and cakes

Biscuits

Preserves

Foreword

Chain Bridge Honey Farm came into being in 1948 when W.S. Robson Senior started a small market garden on the banks of the River Tweed. It was situated near to the Union Chain Bridge, a suspension bridge built in 1820 and thought to be the oldest example of a vehicle-carrying suspension bridge in the world.

Initially soft fruit, laying hens and bees were kept and W.S. Robson took on a job teaching beekeeping in the counties of Berwickshire, Roxburghshire and Selkirkshire. He had been brought up to beekeeping, as his grandfather, a coalminer, kept 60 skeps of honeybees and the family, in common with many country dwellers, had always kept a few hives. W.S. Robson was lucky that he kept company with people who knew a lot more about bees than he did, and so he was able to learn a great deal from those that had the most ability. W.S. Robson Junior was brought up to be a listener in at these discussions and could not help but learn the skills by association.

So, on leaving school in 1962 it was decided to make Chain Bridge Honey Farm into a commercial operation.

Bees were acquired from retiring beekeepers and a workshop set up to manufacture hives out of local timber. Buildings were put up and machinery installed using stainless steel from boat-breakers. All the work was done by employees and helpers using retained profits and gradually the hive numbers were built up to 1800 colonies over a period of fifty years. The bees are all local indigenous black bees and no attempt has been made to 'improve' them.

In 1990 a visitor centre was built to promote the 'brand' and improve cash flow as well as to educate the public about beekeeping. The business employs many people all with their own special skills ranging from woodworking and metalwork right through to making cosmetics and candles. Currently three children of the Robson family and our loyal employees are taking on the future with cautious optimism, as beekeeping has been through some very difficult times recently as a result of an epidemic and some very variable weather. But then commercial beekeeping has always been difficult. Currently we produce between 50 and 60 tons of honey every year, although occasionally the crop is much less, and about 60 'lines' are now distributed to around 400 privately owned shops.

Visitors are most welcome to visit Chain Bridge Honey Farm and get a feeling of this very traditional, stand-alone business. We hope the recipes in this book will inspire you to use locally produced honey in your kitchen.

Introduction

Mention of honey conjures up childhood memories of my father's special comb of heather honey sitting on a plate in the cool larder. His was the first, much anticipated spoonful from the middle of that comb, releasing pools of golden goodness to the plate beneath. This was a special occasion for us because my mother made fresh girdle scones, of which, warm and literally dripping with that wonderful honey, we ate our fill. I can taste it yet.

The honey came from a friend of my father, an Elgin man, David Emslie, who took an old woodman's caravan and cut holes in each side, into which were fitted six beehives. Each year he towed the caravan to where flowers were aplenty – in spring and early summer to meadows filled with clover, later to heather-clad moors. My father's part of the project was to venture inside to ensure there were no 'bee leaks'. 'None,' he confirmed. 'Just a dreadful din!'

The flowers bees forage instil a wealth of flavour. The blossom honey of spring and early summer is light and soft on the palate; later clover adds floral, creamy notes. July and August bring heather honey, a unique, dark amber, thick, viscous honey, full of the woody warm pungency of the moors.

Pure honey is like a fine wine to be savoured and appreciated. Each jar holds many bee miles in its depths, for each bee makes several journeys carrying up to half its weight in pollen and nectar back to the hive. Bees can forage up to eight miles from the hive. On return, they share the location of 'food finds' with other workers by performing a strange 'waggle' dance.

Bees create honey by adding to nectar an enzyme which imparts inbuilt antibacterial properties. They fan the air with their wings to thicken the liquid and prevent bacterial growth.

The oldest evidence of bee products goes back 8,500 years to a site in Turkey where traces of beeswax have been found. The Egyptians prized honey in the kitchen and as medicine; Cleopatra claimed honey was her beauty secret.

The *Book of Proverbs* advises: 'Gracious words are like a honeycomb, sweetness to the soul and health to the body,' and it adds: 'My son, eat honey, for it is good for you, and the drippings of the honeycomb are sweet to your taste.'

In Scotland remains of honey dating back 5,000 years have been identified on pottery found in stone circles on the island of Arran. The original contents of the jars may have been mead or honey beer.

Pollen on a Bronze Age beaker on a Fife burial site suggests an ancient drink from lime honey, flavoured with meadowsweet.

For the Celts honey was an everyday cooking ingredient with game, fish, fruit, nuts, and for making bread, wines and beers, fruit and herbal teas.

Honey was the sweetener used in the kitchen, long before cheaper sugar became available; beekeeping was therefore a common activity. Bees were housed in dome-shaped baskets called skeps until the era of the modern box hive. Demand for beeswax candles was high, particularly from religious orders in the time before the Reformation, so rents and tithes were frequently paid in honey, beeswax or swarms of bees. Interestingly, remains of fifteenth-century stone beehives were discovered on the roof of Rosslyn Chapel during restoration work.

Inevitably bees became associated with folklore and superstition. It was deemed unlucky if a stray swarm of bees landed on property without being claimed. It was also said that, at midnight on Christmas Eve, bees buzz a hymn celebrating the birth of Christ.

Honey has long been known for its healing properties. The book *Healing Threads: Traditional Medicines of the Highlands and Islands* by Mary Beith includes honey-based remedies from the Highlands. She describes a drink to treat coughs made with ground ivy and honey, and tells how gowans (ox-eye daisies) were boiled with honey and applied to heal wounds. Present-day research at Scottish universities has confirmed the effectiveness of honey in killing bacteria that cause wound infections, and the World Health Organisation recommends honey as a natural cough remedy.

Pure honey is valued as a digestive and an antiseptic. The antioxidants it contains are effective in the fight to remove free radicals and promote overall health. Scotland's heather honey is particularly high in these nutrients.

Hay-fever sufferers find relief in taking pure local honey as an antidote to their pollen sensitivity. Honey is a natural skin moisturiser and cleanser and, mixed with fresh lemon juice, makes an invigorating rinse for cleansed hair. To enjoy a spoonful of honey early in the morning can also help your body stay young, fit and able to fight infections.

What does this amazing substance, pure honey, contain? Analysis of one sample showed 18% water, 35% glucose, 40% fructose, 4% other sugars such as sucrose, and the remaining 3% a range of organic acids, minerals, amino acids and proteins.

Industrial, mass-produced honey, which is blended and heated to pasteurise it, will have lost some of its natural food value and taste. Look for honey that is labelled with its origin and name of the beekeeper. The Scottish Beekeepers Association's website (www.scottishbeekeepers. org.uk) will point you in the right direction to find pure full-flavoured Scottish honey, and www.honeybeehive. co.uk/honey/suppliers has a comprehensive list of UK-wide honey suppliers, including of course the Chain Bridge Honey Farm (www.chainbridgehoney.co.uk), making it easy to find pure honey from a hive near where you live.

Honey is a natural emulsifier, thickener and flavour enhancer. It adds moisture to cakes, scones and breads, and imparts colour and flavour to biscuits.

Look after that precious jar of honey and it will look after you. Keep it at room temperature to prevent crystallisation. Heating destroys much of its goodness, so enjoy it straight from the jar when possible.

A jar of pure honey in the store cupboard is an invaluable ingredient. Honey is *the* hidden jewel of Scotland's rich larder.

The recipes in this book provide simple ways to enjoy the richness of honey – in sauces and soups, in scones and shortbreads, in porridge and puddings. There are classic recipes, like Tattie Drottle and Scots Toasts, and traditional ones with a twist, like Sticky Honey Pudding and Honey Mincemeat. There are also modern ones, like Whisky Honey Prawns and Fresh Fruit, Lemon and Honey Drizzle Cake, and the occasional historic one too, such as a medieval Potage of Honey-Spiced Salmon.

The recipes are graded according to ease of making, with one bee being simple, two for intermediate, and three requiring more advanced skills. There are also hints and tips and ideas to encourage everyone to use honey more often in day-to-day cooking.

Breakfast

'In the breakfast,' said Dr Johnson, 'the Scots must be confessed to excel. The tea and coffee are accompanied not only with butter, but with honey, conserves, and marmalades.'

(From the *Journal* written by his friend, Scotsman James Boswell, of their Scottish tour in 1771.)

Traditional oatmeal porridge

'Through that magic cauldron, the porridge pot, Scottish oatmeal has been transmuted through the centuries into Scottish brains and brawn.' – F. Marian McNeill, *The Scots Kitchen.*

In Scotland it is the tradition to stir porridge with a stick known as a *spurtle* or *theevil*. The Druids believed it was lucky to stir clockwise, but no matter, stirring is important. There are as many styles of porridge as there are types of oats. I like to use fine or medium Scottish oatmeal, milled by Hamlyns at Portsoy not far from my home. A rougher porridge is achieved by using pinhead oatmeal, which it is better to soak. Soaking oatmeal in water overnight helps release nutrients, aids digestion and speeds the cooking process in the morning.

45g (1½oz) medium-fine oatmeal per person
300ml (½ pint) cold water
¼ teaspoon sea salt

Put the oatmeal in a pan with the water. Stir over a medium heat till the porridge thickens and boils, reduce the heat to simmer and keep stirring. The porridge will cook in 4 or 5 minutes. Add sea salt just before serving.

'Ladle straight into cold porringers or soup plates and serve with individual bowls of cream, or milk, or buttermilk. Each spoonful of porridge, which should be very hot, is dipped in the cream which should be quite cold, before it is conveyed to the mouth.'
– F. Marian McNeill, *The Scots Kitchen*.

My grandfather ate porridge from a large soup plate. He poured cold cream from a small matching jug over each hot spoonful.

'Children often like a layer of sugar, honey, syrup, or treacle, or of raw oatmeal on top. To encourage her reluctant young porridge-eaters a nurse used to draw a golden dromedary with syrup on the surface. By the time the dromedary was eaten, the porridge too, had vanished.' – F. Marian McNeill, *The Scots Kitchen*.

More adventurous porridge eaters may like to draw a honey bee on theirs!

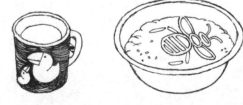

Posh porridge

My friend Colin, who owned a bed and breakfast in
Freuchie, Fife, transformed traditional oatmeal porridge
into 'Posh porridge' by adding:

---

1 or 2 teaspoons pure honey
¼ level teaspoon ground cinnamon and ginger
A handful of raisins or sultanas

I made this recipe in my grandmother's jam pan to feed
folk at The Big Tent weekend in Fife. It was so popular
the pan was refilled many times that day.

Honey granolas

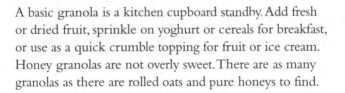

A basic granola is a kitchen cupboard standby. Add fresh
or dried fruit, sprinkle on yoghurt or cereals for breakfast,
or use as a quick crumble topping for fruit or ice cream.
Honey granolas are not overly sweet. There are as many
granolas as there are rolled oats and pure honeys to find.

Crunchy honey granola

I like to use gluten-free jumbo oats to make a chunky crisp granola.

180g (generous 6oz) jumbo oats
30g (1oz) ground flax seeds
60g (2oz) sunflower seeds
60g (2oz) pumpkin seeds
40ml (2½ tablespoons) pure honey, warmed to soften
40ml (2½ tablespoons) oil

Turn on the oven at 150°C (fan 130°C), 300°F, Gas 2. Choose a wide flat baking tray to let the granola spread and allow it to cook evenly; line the tray with baking foil. Put all the ingredients into a bowl and mix together. Pour onto the tray and spread evenly. Bake for 30 minutes, turning at regular intervals. Keep an eye on the granola – there is little time difference between crisply baked and burnt! Cool and store in a jar or tub with a tight-fitting lid. Keep for up to two months. I find it only lasts a few days!

Heather honey granola

Heather honey adds a distinctive tang.

Bake as the above recipe, substituting regular rolled oats and pure heather honey. Reduce the baking time to 24 minutes, however, because the lighter oats and heather honey will take less time to crisp.

Compôte of autumn fruits

My mother spent hours simmering, then pouring hot autumn fruit and berries into heavy Kilner jars. They were sealed, labelled and stored for the winter in the cool larder. Now all we need do is cook, cool and freeze.

---

4 or 5 eating apples, Cox's or Russet have a good sharp tang
2 Bramley or similar cooking apples
225g (8oz) plums, washed, stoned and quartered
225g (8oz) brambles or other autumn berries, washed and hulled
1 small fresh orange
Cinnamon stick (optional)
1 dessertspoon of pure honey

Peel, core and slice the apples and put into a deep pan along with the plums and autumn berries. Wash the skin of the orange or lemon. Pare a thin long strip of orange peel, squeeze the juice and add both to the pan with the cinnamon. Bring to the boil, stir, reduce the heat to simmer and cover the pan. Leave to cook slowly for 15 to 20 minutes. Stir in the honey when warm, then cool completely. Pour into suitable containers, seal and label. Freeze for up to three months. This quantity will make approximately 675g (1½lb) depending on the size of the apples.

'Heather Honey is an ingredient in such classic drinks as Drambuie and Atholl Brose, as well as in cakes. With orange marmalade it should appear on every Scottish breakfast table where the old traditions are cherished.'
– F. Marian McNeill, *The Scots Kitchen*.

CINNAMON – OPTIONAL

Savouries and Snacks

Scots toasts

'Of these there are many varieties.'
– F. Marian McNeill, *The Scots Kitchen*.

A period afternoon tea inspired by baking from past eras is held at Skaill House, Orkney, in September each year. I have the pleasure of doing recipe research for this and often refer to the writings of Orkney-born F. Marian McNeill, from which I discovered 'Scots Toasts'.

Originally served on rounds of buttered toast or fried bread, these make an ideal canapé spread on oatcakes or small savoury biscuits.

Finnan toasts

Heather honey enhances the sweet smokiness of the haddock.

Serves up to 10 as a starter or canapé
115g (4oz) butter
350g (12oz) naturally smoked haddock fillet. Ask your fishmonger
    for broken pieces – they will be cheaper to buy.
1 tablespoon double cream (optional)
3 or 4 teaspoons fresh lemon juice
1 teaspoon pure Scottish heather honey
Ground black pepper to taste

Melt the butter in a pan and add the fish. Stir to cook, breaking the flesh into flakes with the back of a wooden spoon. The fish turns opaque quickly, when you should turn off the heat. Stir in the cream, lemon juice and honey and season to taste with freshly ground black pepper. Haddock is salted before smoking, so added salt is not required. Pour into a container, seal and store in the fridge. Remove from the fridge to soften 30 minutes before serving. Spread on small oatcakes or savoury biscuits garnished with a sprinkle of chopped parsley. Keeps up to four days and freezes for up to two months.

Potted cheese and ale

I use mature Orkney cheddar for its robust flavour. Smoked Orkney cheddar lends mellowness boosted by a spoon of heather honey. More adventurous 'cheese potters' can choose from a variety of flavoured mature cheddars such as sweet chilli or red onion.

Serves up to 10 as a canapé
115g (4oz) mature Orkney cheddar cheese
115g (4oz) smoked Orkney cheddar
1 bottle Scapa Special beer or similar 4.2% pale ale
1 teaspoon English mustard
2 teaspoons Worcester sauce
Generous pinch of cayenne pepper
1 teaspoon pure heather honey

Whizz the cheese in a food processor, gradually adding enough beer to make a smooth spreadable paste. Beat in 1 teaspoon mustard, 2 teaspoons of Worcester sauce, a pinch of cayenne pepper and 1 teaspoon of heather honey.

Store in the fridge in a sealed container for up to one month. For a rougher spread, mix grated cheese with the other ingredients in a bowl with a wooden spoon. Spread onto thin oatcakes with a garnish of parsley and slivers of tomato.

MATURE ORKNEY CHEDDAR

Honey
PURE SCOTTISH
HEATHER
HONEY

Chicken salmagundi

A recipe from a Victorian cookbook was the idea behind this unusual 'Scots toast'. Honey complements the citrus notes.

Serves 10 people
175g (6oz) cooked chicken breast
Sea salt
Ground black pepper
1 level teaspoon English mustard
1 level teaspoon grated horseradish, available ready prepared in most
    supermarkets
1 teaspoon grated orange zest
1 teaspoon grated lemon zest
Fresh lemon juice to taste
1 tablespoon mayonnaise
1 teaspoon pure honey
1 dessertspoon finely chopped spring onions or chives

Whizz the cooked chicken in a food processor: season with sea salt, ground black pepper and 1 level teaspoon each of mustard and horseradish. Add orange and lemon zest with fresh lemon juice to taste. Lastly beat in the mayonnaise, heather honey and chopped spring onions or chives. Store in a sealed container and chill till required. Keep up to three days in the fridge. Serve on oatcakes and savoury biscuits, garnished with a slice of pickled gherkin and sprig of parsley. Makes a tasty sandwich filling and tastes good in a baked potato.

Pokerounce spice mix

Medieval cooks used strong flavourings to disguise questionable food! Pokerounce was one of their mixes.

1 tablespoon rough ground black pepper
1 tablespoon ground cinnamon
1 tablespoon ground ginger

Mix the spices and keep in a small tub or jar. I like to add it to gingerbreads and fruit loaves.

Pokerounce-spiced honey

60g (2oz) pure honey
4 to 8 teaspoons of pokerounce spice mix

Add 4 to 8 teaspoons of spice mix according to taste and stir well.

Store in a jar with a tight-fitting lid.

A jar of pokerounce-spiced honey has many culinary uses. Spread on hot buttered toast. Rub over beef, lamb, pork or gammon, gammon steaks, chops, chicken, turkey steaks or salmon fillets before grilling, roasting or baking. Stir into yoghurt, add to fresh and stewed fruits, pour over ice cream.

Starters

Honey-Spiced beetroot.

Prawns with whisky and honey.

Prawns with whisky and honey

Sri Lankan food writer Priya Wickramasinghe presented a master-class on her native cookery during Orkney International Science Festival. One dish required fresh prawns, so Dougie Stanger of Kirkwall Bay Shellfish contacted local fishing boats direct. Prawns caught at 8 a.m. in Scapa Flow were in Priya's wok by 11 a.m. that morning. Now, that's fresh! A friend gave me the idea for this recipe from one she researched for foodie friends.

Serves 4 as a starter
350g (12oz) fresh prawns shelled and de-veined
125g (4½oz) pure honey
Zest and juice of 1 lime
2 tablespoons whisky
Chilli flakes
Vegetable oil

Turn on the oven at 200°C (fan 180°C), 400°F, Gas 6. Line a roasting tin with foil and oil well. Mix 100g of honey with 1 tablespoon of lime juice and the same of whisky. Lay the prawns flat in the tin, pour the honey mix over, toss to coat and scatter with chilli flakes. Bake 10 minutes till pink and firm; do not overcook.

Remove from the oven, pour excess juices into a pan with the rest of the honey, lime zest and juice and whisky.

Simmer to reduce to a syrupy consistency and use a little to glaze the warm prawns. Serve the prawns in warm bowls with the remaining sauce in a jug on the side. A rocket salad and crusty bread are all that is needed to accompany this. It is equally good served cold; the sauce thickens as it cools. Salmon glazed and baked with the sauce is delicious.

Heather honey-cured salmon

Recently a friend kindly brought me a fresh Kirkwall Bay salmon on a return journey from Orkney, so, after filleting and de-boning, I thought to create a honey cure. The combination of salmon and heather honey creates subtle soft flavours, well worth the three-day wait.

Serves 4
100g (3½oz) rough sea salt ground with a mortar and pestle
A few grinds of black pepper
115g (4oz) pure Scottish heather honey
225g (8oz) salmon fillet

Mix the honey, salt and pepper together. Line a suitable dish with baking foil and line the foil with cling film. Spread half of the mix on the base of the dish. Cover with the salmon, skin side down, then spread the rest of the mix over the fish and wrap tightly in the cling film and then the foil, forming a neat parcel. Lay a plate or dish on top which is to hold heavy weights such as tins or jars to press onto the parcel. Chill for three days in the fridge, turning each day.

Remove from the wrapping, wash in cold water and dry on paper towel. Slice thinly. Store in a sealed container in the fridge for up to 5 days.

Serve with rocket leaves and a slice of fresh lemon and honey-spiced beetroot on the side.

Honey-spiced beetroot

Several years ago, I discovered the Moroccan spice mix *ras el hanout* in an Egyptian spice market. Since then it has become more widely available in this country. The aromatic mix of spices, herbs, rose and lavender petals adds spice and warmth.

Serves 6 to 8
280g (10oz) grated cooked beetroot
2 teaspoons *ras el hanout* spice mix
15ml (1 tablespoon) balsamic vinegar
25g (scant 1oz) pure Scottish heather honey
Sea salt to season

Mix the ingredients in a bowl, season very lightly with a little sea salt, chill and serve with heather honey-cured salmon or other smoked fish or meats. Store in a sealed container in the fridge for up to a week. This is excellent with cheeses.

Soups

'Beautiful Soup, so rich and green,
Waiting in a hot tureen!
Who for such dainties would not stoop?
Soup of the evening, beautiful Soup!'

from Lewis Carroll,
Alice in Wonderland

The Mock Turtle.
Lewis Carrol's
Alice in Wonderland
apologies to J. Tennial

Soup of the Evening
Beautiful Soup!

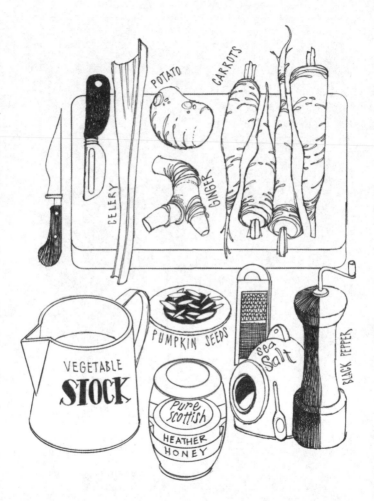

CELERY

POTATO

CARROTS

GINGER

PUMPKIN SEEDS

VEGETABLE **STOCK**

Pure Scottish HEATHER HONEY

Sea Salt

BLACK PEPPER

Carrot and ginger soup with a hint of honey

I love the sweet spice of ginger and honey in this soup. In less than half an hour a steaming plateful is ready to enjoy.

Serves 4

500g (1lb 2oz) carrots, peeled and chopped
1 stick of celery, cleaned and chopped
1 medium potato, peeled and chopped
1 tablespoon grated root ginger
1.2 litres (2 pints) vegetable stock or water
1 level teaspoon sea salt
Ground black pepper
2 teaspoons pure Scottish heather honey
1 tablespoon pumpkin seeds

Put the vegetables, ginger, salt and stock into a deep pan and bring to the boil. Reduce the heat, cover and simmer for 15 minutes till the vegetables are tender, adding more liquid if needed. Blend till smooth, stir in 2 teaspoons of heather honey, taste and adjust the seasoning.

Heat a small frying pan and toast the pumpkin seeds till they pop.

Serve the soup in heated bowls with toasted pumpkin seeds scattered on top.

Tattie drottle

I enjoyed working in the canteen at Baxters of Speyside where, despite making soup all day, the staff still appreciated a bowl of steaming homemade soup at lunch time. Doris, one of the cooks, had an endless supply of recipes and this is one of the all-time favourites.

Serves 4
30g (1oz) butter
600g (1lb 5oz) floury potatoes, peeled and sliced
1 onion, peeled and sliced
1.2 litres (2 pints) vegetable or chicken stock
1 celery stalk, cleaned and chopped
2 teaspoons pure heather honey
Pinch of nutmeg
1 level teaspoon sea salt
A few pinches of white pepper if you have any
300ml (½ pint) creamy milk

Put the butter, potatoes and onions into a deep soup pan and cook very slowly for 5 minutes on low heat, stirring to prevent sticking and browning. Add the stock, celery, honey and seasoning and boil, then reduce the heat, cover and simmer for 20 minutes. Using a potato masher, roughly mash together, stir in the milk and heat to simmer, taste and adjust the seasoning if needed. Serve hot with warm, freshly baked oatcakes crushed over the soup to make a filling meal.

Vegetables

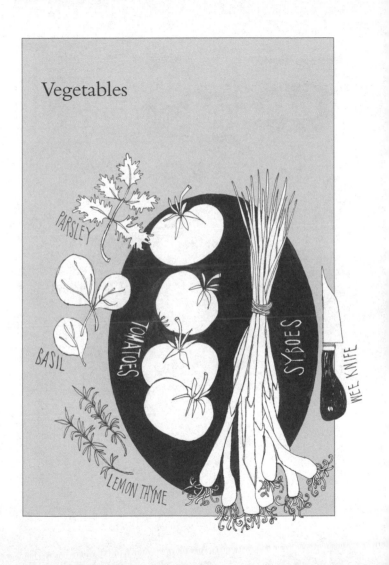

PARSLEY

BASIL

LEMON THYME

TOMATOES

SYBOES

WEE KNIFE

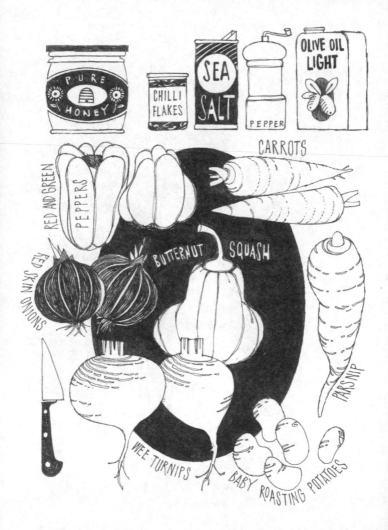

Honey-roasted vegetables

My friend Su introduced me to honey-roasted vegetables. Another friend, Doreen, makes a meal by laying honey-coated seasoned chicken breast fillets, lamb or pork chops or salmon fillets on top halfway through cooking.

Serves 4 people
2 large carrots, peeled and cut into chunks
1 large parsnip, peeled and cut into chunks
2 red skinned onions, peeled and cut into quarters
1 red and 1 green pepper, de-seeded, cored and cut into chunks
2 or 3 small turnips, peeled and quartered.
1 butternut squash, peeled, de-seeded and cut into chunks
225g (8oz) baby roasting potatoes, scrubbed

For the honey coating:
2 tablespoons pure honey
2 tablespoons light olive, rapeseed or sunflower oil
1 level teaspoon sea salt
Freshly ground black pepper
A sprinkling of chilli flakes (optional)

Oven temperature 200°C (fan 180°C), 400°F, Gas 6. Line a roasting tin with foil. Mix the vegetables and coating ingredients in a bowl. Tip into the roasting tin, sprinkle with chilli flakes if liked. Roast 35 to 40 minutes, turning once halfway through cooking (add meat, chicken or fish at this point). Serve hot with roasts and grills; a good base for soup or pasta sauce.

A dish of summer vegetables

This recipe conjures up childhood memories of our back garden, picking peas, mother thinning rows of carrots, my sister gathering runner beans; then scrubbing, topping, tailing and shelling. Mum made this with young vegetables from the garden.

Serves 4

2 knobs of soft butter

225g (8oz) young carrots, scrubbed and trimmed. We used the small carrots thinned from the rows, so left them whole. Cut larger carrots into thick slices.

115g (4oz) fresh shelled peas

115g (4oz) shelled broad beans, picked when they are small and sweet

2 or 3 white new spring turnips, peeled and cut into chunks

115g (4oz) young runner beans, topped, tailed and chopped

(Any young vegetables being thinned from the garden can go into this dish.)

1 level teaspoon sea salt

1 generous teaspoon pure honey

Chopped fresh parsley

Fresh lemon juice

Turn on the oven at 180°C (fan 160°C), 350°F, Gas 4. Take an oven-proof dish, rub with a knob of butter and toss in the vegetables, season with sea salt, add the honey and another knob of butter. Pour in boiling water to just cover the vegetables, lay a sheet of greaseproof paper over

the dish and cover with a lid. The paper seals in the
flavours and keeps the lid clean.

Put into a deep tray and oven-bake for 35 to 40
minutes. Remove from the oven, lift the lid carefully:
steam can burn. Drain, retain the juices to use as stock.
Return the vegetables to the dish, toss with lemon juice
mixed with a little honey and chopped parsley, then
enjoy.

YOUNG CARROTS

SHELLED PEAS

SHELLED BROAD BEANS

NEW SPRING TURNIPS

YOUNG RUNNER BEANS

SEA SALT

BUTTER

BUTTER SALT

LEMON JUICE

CHOPPED FRESH PARSLEY

PURE HONEY

HONEY

Tomato and syboe salad

Syboe is Scots for spring onion, derived from the French *ciboule*. This is a simple tomato and onion salad, but when Scottish tomatoes are at their best it cannot be beaten.

Serves 4

450g (1lb) ripe Scottish tomatoes, thinly sliced
1 bunch of spring onions (syboes), washed, trimmed and finely
    chopped
Fresh garden herbs: parsley, basil or lemon thyme, finely chopped

For the dressing:
2 tablespoons extra virgin olive oil or rapeseed oil
1 tablespoon apple cider vinegar
2 teaspoons pure honey
1 level teaspoon mustard powder
Sea salt
Freshly ground black pepper

Arrange overlapping slices of tomatoes layered with the onions and herbs in a wide flat dish. Pour the dressing ingredients into a jam jar with a tight-fitting lid and shake vigorously to mix. Pour the dressing over the salad, leave to marinate for 10 minutes and serve.

Main Meals

Potage of honey-spiced salmon

Elizabethan and medieval cooks relied on the use of strong flavours. The skilled use of vinegar, garlic and spices created dishes which are, to our tastebuds, 'sweet and savoury'. This dish, based on a medieval pie filling, was served in traditional style to 300 people at a medieval banquet which took place during Orkney International Science Festival in the Bishop's Palace in Kirkwall, Orkney. Parents of otherwise non-fish-eating children reported it was a great success.

Spice-mix for fish
A 'Gode Spice' to season fish. Add to rich cakes as an alternative to the usual spices.

Mix together:
½ teaspoon ground nutmeg
1 teaspoon ground cardamom (optional)
1 teaspoon ground ginger
½ teaspoon ground black pepper
½ teaspoon ground cinnamon

Store in an airtight, labelled container.

Serves 8 to 10

To pickle the fish
1kg salmon filleted
300ml (½ pint) white wine or cider vinegar
300ml (½ pint) dry white wine
1 teaspoon of whole black peppercorns
1 or 2 bay leaves
Pinch of saffron or turmeric (optional)

Put the wine, vinegar, pepper and saffron into a pan, add
the fish and bring to a simmering boil. Cover, simmer
gently, turning once, for 10 to 15 minutes till firm. Turn
off the heat and cool. Leave in a cool place overnight.
The next day drain the cooked fish, remove bones, skin
etc., and put into a large bowl.

Potage of pickled fish

Mix together:
4 apples, peeled cored and finely chopped
2 pears, peeled cored and finely chopped
5 fresh plums, stoned and finely chopped
300ml (½ pint) white wine
1 dessertspoon pure honey
2 teaspoons spice mix
5 prunes chopped
5 dates chopped
A handful of raisins

Add:
Flaked salmon
Sea salt

To serve:
Chopped parsley, tarragon and dill

Mix the ingredients together in a large bowl; fold in the flaked salmon, season to taste with sea salt and add more honey and spices if liked. Serve chilled in a large earthenware bowl garnished with freshly chopped herbs. Fronds of fresh dill add an authentic touch.

Chicken stovies (Poulet Béarnaise)

Scottish cooking is described by F. Marian McNeill in *The Scots Kitchen* as 'pastoral cooking, brightly influenced by old ties with France'. My friend Veronica gave me this recipe. Her father, a professor of French, provided her with plenty of opportunities to collect authentic recipes during the family's annual holiday in France. It is a French haute cuisine version of the Highland recipe for chicken stovies – however 'poulet Béarnaise' sounds more exotic.

Serves 4

450g (1lb) chicken joints, legs and thighs, skinned and trimmed, or 4 large skinned chicken breast fillets, cut along their length into 4 pieces each

1 large carrot, peeled and grated

4 medium-sized potatoes, peeled and grated

1 large onion, peeled and finely chopped

1 large eating apple, peeled, cored and grated

Sea salt and ground black pepper

For the sauce:

20g (¾oz) pure Scottish heather honey

30ml (2 tablespoons) cider vinegar

120ml (¼ pint) dry white wine

300ml (10fl oz) chicken stock or hot water

Turn on the oven at 150°C (fan 130°C), 300°F, Gas 2.
Layer the chicken and vegetables in a deep casserole dish.
Lightly season each layer with sea salt and ground black
pepper. Mix the sauce ingredients, pour over, cover and
bake for 1 to 1½ hours till tender and the vegetables are
melting.

Season to taste and stir in more liquid if needed.
Serve with chunks of fresh crusty bread to mop the
juices.

Vary the dish with chopped smoked bacon in the
layers, or bake with lean pork steak, adding more grated
apple and a pinch of ground cloves.

Poulet Béarnaise

Chicken Stovies

Honey–roasted gammon

My neighbour Aubrey is famous among his friends for delicious honey-roasted gammon. No matter how I try I can never quite match his expertise. This is the special recipe.

Serves 6 to 8

2kg (4½lbs) rolled gammon
2 litres (3½ pints) cider
2 tablespoons wholegrain mustard
2 tablespoons pure honey
Handful of whole cloves
1 tin (approximately 510g, 8 halves) halved peaches

The day before, choose a container deep enough to hold the gammon comfortably. Pour over sufficient cider to cover and leave in a cool dry place overnight. The following day, turn on the oven at 160°C (fan 140°C), 325°F, Gas 3.

Lay the gammon in a roasting tin. Make a paste of 1 tablespoon each of wholegrain mustard and honey and rub well over the surface of the gammon. Pour in a little of the soaking juices, retaining the remainder to baste the gammon during cooking. Cover the roasting tin with foil and put into the oven to roast for 2 hours. Baste occasionally, adding more cider if needed. Remove from

the oven. Turn up the heat to 200°C (fan 180°C), 400°F, Gas 6. Remove the skin and take care, it will be hot. Score the fat in parallel lines in one direction, then score parallel lines across at an angle to create a diamond pattern.

Make more honey-mustard mixture to rub over the gammon, and stud each cut fat diamond with a clove. Roast for 25 to 30 minutes. For the last 15 minutes add a tin of halved peaches plus their juice. Rest for 20 to 30 minutes before carving, adding a peach to each helping. Strain the juice from the roasting tin and serve this as 'gravy'. The gammon is good served cold.

Shehed Qismat masala

Chicken Tikka Masala has been voted the most popular new Scottish dish. It was invented in Glasgow by Ali Ahmed Aslam of the Shish Mahal restaurant. One of the diners one evening complained that the Chicken Tikka was too dry, so it went back to the kitchen where a tin of tomato soup was transformed into a spiced sauce to moisten the dish. It was greatly appreciated, so much so that now every Indian restaurant has created their own version. The Qismat restaurant in Elgin near my home is owned and run by Mr Liaqat Ali and his family. Mr Ali's son, Atif, kindly created this tikka masala recipe, shehed qismat masala, for the *Honey Bible* using pure honey as an ingredient. *Shehed* means honey in Urdu, and *masala* a mixture of spices.

Serves 6 to 8

For the chicken marinade:
675g (1½lb) boneless, skinless chicken breasts
125g (4½oz) whole-milk Greek-style yoghurt
1 tablespoon pure honey
2 tablespoons vegetable oil
2 teaspoons fresh lime or fresh lemon juice
1 large clove of garlic, minced
1 teaspoon sea salt
1 red chilli, finely chopped

MARINADE

VEG OIL

SHEHED HONEY

BONELESS SKINLESS CHICKEN FILLETS

SEA SALT

GREEK STYLE Yoghurt

LEMON OR LIME JUICE

CLOVE OF GARLIC

RED CHILLI

SEA SALT

P

SAUCE

UNSALTED butter

TOMATO PUREE

GINGER

GREEN PEPPER

WHITE ONION

GROUND CORIANDER

GROUND CUMIN

GROUND CARDAMOM

GROUND NUTMEG

PAPRIKA

CAYENNE PEPPER

WATER

PURE HONEY

DOUBLE CREAM

CORIANDER

56

For the sauce:
1 tablespoon ground coriander
1½ teaspoons ground cumin
½ teaspoon ground cardamom
½ teaspoon ground nutmeg
1½ teaspoons paprika
½ teaspoon cayenne pepper
1 tablespoon grated peeled fresh ginger
4 tablespoons unsalted butter
1 green pepper, de-seeded and chopped
1 large white onion, finely chopped
150ml (5oz) tomato puree
100ml (3½fl oz) water
120ml (4fl oz) double cream or half and half with water
1¼ teaspoons sea salt
½ teaspoon black pepper
15g (½oz) pure honey
2 tablespoons chopped fresh coriander to garnish

———————————

Use a fork to prick the chicken breasts all over on both sides. Cut the chicken into small bite–size chunks. In a bowl whisk the marinade ingredients together, add the chicken and rub the mixture well over the meat, cover and lay aside to marinade for at least 2 hours. To make the sauce, mix the coriander, cumin, cardamom, paprika, cayenne and grated ginger in a bowl. Melt the butter in a sauté pan over medium heat and cook the onions slowly, stirring till they are light brown and caramelised, about 5 minutes. Reduce the heat and stir in the spice mixture. Add the green pepper, tomato puree, water, cream, salt

and pepper and bring the sauce to the boil. Lower
the heat to simmer uncovered to reduce slightly for
10 minutes. Stir to prevent the sauce sticking.

Cook the chicken breasts with the marinade in a
heated frying pan, turning a few times. Lower the heat if
they char too quickly. It takes 6 to 8 minutes till the
chicken is cooked through and browned well on both
sides. Add the chicken to the simmering sauce along with
the honey and simmer, stirring occasionally, for 5
minutes. Taste and adjust the seasoning. Remove the pan
from the heat and serve sprinkled with fresh coriander
and accompanied by warm naan bread, boiled or pilau
rice and a light salad of fresh leaves, chopped red onion,
cucumber and mint.

Warm spiced-honey beef salad

My maternal great-grandfathers were master butchers. One, John Cruickshank, was a butcher at Rosemount in Aberdeen. The other, Thomas Ritchie, bred Aberdeen Angus cattle at Inchyra farm to supply his butchery and slaughterhouse in Grangemouth nearby. He called them his black beauties.

Locally bred, quality Scottish beef is still on my family menu. Plainly cooked, a spiced honey dressing is all that is needed to finish the dish.

Serves 2

4 teaspoons pokerounce spice mix (see page 30)
30g (1oz) pure honey
225g (8oz) lean rump or sirloin steak cut into strips
15g (½oz) cornflour
Sea salt
Freshly ground black pepper
30g (1oz) coconut oil
2 cloves fresh garlic, crushed

For the topping:
1 tablespoon jumbo oat flakes
Sea salt
Freshly ground black pepper

Make the spiced honey by mixing 4 teaspoons of poker-ounce spice mix with the honey, cover and lay aside.

Put the cornflour in a strong poly bag, season with sea salt and ground black pepper. Add the steak, hold the top of the bag tightly and shake vigorously. Put the coated meat strips onto a plate beside the cooker. Take a wok or deep frying pan, add half the coconut oil, heat to melt, add 1 crushed clove of garlic, stir to flavour the oil and remove when browning. Separate the steak strips with clean fingers, laying half quickly into the hot oil and stir to colour and seal. The meat will cook quickly. Test with the point of a skewer or sharp knife; try not to overcook. Reduce the heat, drizzle with 2 teaspoons of spiced honey, stir and toss into a heated bowl. Repeat with the rest of the steak.

Wipe the cooking pan and pour in the oats, toss to toast, season with salt and pepper and remove from the heat.

Arrange the hot beef on warmed plates, scatter with toasted oats and serve with a large tossed green salad, for example tomato and syboe salad (see page 46) and new potatoes or crusty bread and butter.

Or would you prefer a sauce? Add 150ml (¼ pint) stock or water to the cooking juices in the pan. Mix two teaspoons of cornflour to a paste with water. Stir this into the liquids and heat till it thickens and boils, add the cooked steak and stir. Taste, adjust the seasoning, and serve with boiled rice or noodles and steamed broccoli.

Puddings

Morayshire apples

In 1950 the Benedictine monks at Pluscarden Abbey near
Elgin established a heritage apple orchard. The apple
collection now has over 100 varieties suited to growing
conditions in the North East. The monks make apple
juice, cook and freeze the apples and, naturally, enjoy
them freshly picked. Brother Michael de Klerk is the
apple expert, and he has assured me that some of the
current crop will find its way into a dish of Morayshire
apples forthwith.

Serves 4 to 6
450g (1lb) cooking apples, peeled cored and sliced
60g (2oz) pure honey
4 tablespoons (60ml) water
Pinch of ground cloves (if liked)

For the topping:
115g (4oz) medium oatmeal
60g (2oz) chopped suet
60g (2oz) chopped hazelnuts
60g (2oz) soft brown sugar
60g (2oz) pure honey, warmed

Turn on the oven at 180°C (fan 160°C), 350°F, Gas 4.
Stew the apples with the honey, water and cloves till soft,
and put them into a suitable oven-proof dish. Mix the
oatmeal, suet, hazelnuts and soft brown sugar to make the

topping. Spread evenly over the apples.

Bake for 35 to 45 minutes till golden and crisp. Pour the warm honey over the pudding before serving hot with custard or fresh cream.

Bramble and apple frushie

Several years ago my friend Alison's son James spied an elderly gentleman using a clever 'hands-free' bramble-picking kit. Wasting no time, he went home and produced kits for his mum and friends. Take a rectangular 2-litre ice-cream container, punch a hole in each end, near the rim, thread a length of thick string through so that it will hang round the neck to waist level, then secure each end with a knot. It is brilliant.

Frushie, a Scots word for 'crumbly', aptly describes the pastry part of this delicious tart.

Serves 4
1 shallow pie dish or flan dish, 20cm (8in) diameter, well oiled
225g (8oz) cooking apples, cored, peeled and sliced
115g (4oz) brambles, cleaned
60g (2oz) pure honey, warmed
3 teaspoons rose water
1 egg beaten
Caster or icing sugar

For the pastry:
225g (8oz) plain flour, sifted
115g (4oz) butter or margarine
Pinch of salt
Cold water
(Alternatively use ready-made shortcrust pastry.)

BRAMBLE AND APPLE FRUSHIE

Turn on the oven at 200°C (fan 180°C), 400°F, Gas 6, and oil the pie dish. Gently simmer the fruit in a saucepan till soft, reserving sufficient apple slices to lay overlapping on top of the cooked fruit. Sift the flour and salt into a bowl, rub in the butter or margarine and mix to a pliable, smooth dough with cold water. Rest the pastry for 5 minutes.

Roll out the pastry on a floured board and line the dish. Knead the scraps, roll out again and cut into strips to decorate the top of the tart. Pour the stewed fruit into the pastry case and spread evenly. Lay the apple slices overlapping each other on top of the fruit. Mix the rose water with the warm honey and pour over the fruit. Dampen the pastry edges with water and decorate the top with a lattice design of pastry strips, pressing each end into the damp pastry to secure. Glaze the strips with beaten egg and put the dish onto a tray to catch any drips. Bake for 25 to 30 minutes till golden.

Dust with caster or icing sugar, and serve warm with cream, custard or ice cream.

Sticky honey pudding

From a recipe by Chef Michael Stitt of the Carmoor Guest House in Carrbridge, where I stay in October while taking part in the annual World Porridge Championships, the Golden Spurtle. It is a home from home.

Sticky toffee pudding made with pure honey is light in texture and on the palate.

Serves 8

175g (6oz) stoned dates
200ml (7fl oz) boiling water
¾ teaspoon bicarbonate of soda
½ teaspoon vanilla essence
2 teaspoons instant coffee dissolved in a little water
75g (3oz) butter
75g (2½oz) caster sugar
75g (2½oz) pure honey, warmed
2 eggs, beaten
175g (6oz) self-raising flour

For the sauce:

115g (4oz) butter
115g (4oz) pure honey
6 tablespoons double cream

Turn on the oven at 170°C (fan 150°C), 325°F, Gas 3. Oil a large 1.2-litre (2-pint) oven-proof dish. Put the dates in a bowl, add boiling water, bicarbonate of soda, vanilla

essence, dissolved coffee and stir. Cream the caster sugar and butter till light, then beat in the honey and eggs. Fold in the flour and date mixture; the mixture will be sloppy. Pour into the dish. Bake for 30 to 40 minutes till risen and firm. Check after 30 minutes.

Meanwhile, make the sauce. Heat the ingredients on medium heat, stirring till the mixture thickens a little, cool. Pour the sauce over the hot pudding and serve with cream, ice cream or custard.

Rhubarb

The first rhubarb of the season is called the 'Spring Conditioner', because it is good for digestion.

In the 1980s, I worked in Edinburgh, where I lived with my elderly Aunt Gladys in her flat at Comely Bank. At the door to the garden was a small plot where Gladys had planted a crown of rhubarb, over which a zinc bucket was placed to force growth. I came home one evening to find my dear aunt on a chair, camouflaged by refuse bins, at the door of the garden guarding the rhubarb, so concerned was she that another tenant might steal the first picking!

Cook rhubarb, adding honey to soften any acid flavours.

NEIGHBOURHOOD
RHUBARB
WATCH

Rhubarb fool

Fool is from the old Scottish word *foull*, derived from the French *fouler*, meaning 'to press'. Cooked fruit is rubbed through a sieve to remove seeds and skin, hence the name. Rhubarb and honey make a fool which is not overly sweet.

Serves 4
450g (1lb) rhubarb, cleaned and chopped
85g (3oz) pure honey
2 tablespoons water
220g (7½oz) thick Greek yoghurt
150ml (¼ pint) double cream, whipped thickly
150ml (¼ pint) custard (use ready-made, it is so handy)

Cook the rhubarb with the honey and water till tender. Cool. Pass through a sieve or process till smooth. Pour into a bowl with the other ingredients and fold together. Serve chilled.

Cream crowdie

This recipe appears in a book by F. Marian McNeill called *Hallowe'en: Its Origin, Rites and Ceremonies in the Scottish Tradition*, in which the last chapter describes traditional treats from her Orkney childhood.

Similar to cranachan, cream crowdie is easier to make, and can be shaped by the cook's imagination, depending on season and occasion.

Serves 4
150ml (¼ pint) double cream
Oatmeal, lightly toasted in the oven or under a low grill
15g (½oz) pure honey
A few drops of vanilla essence (if liked)

Whip the cream and honey together till softly thick, and add a few drops of vanilla essence. Beat in a handful of toasted oatmeal to stiffen the cream but leaving it still of a consistency to pipe. Add a spoon or two of Drambuie for special occasions.

To serve: in the summer, fold in chopped soft fruits and chill. In the autumn, fold in stewed brambles and apples and chill. At Christmas, beat in mincemeat and freeze till the mixture is like a soft ice-cream dessert.

It also makes a topping for carrot cake, cup-cakes and shortbread.

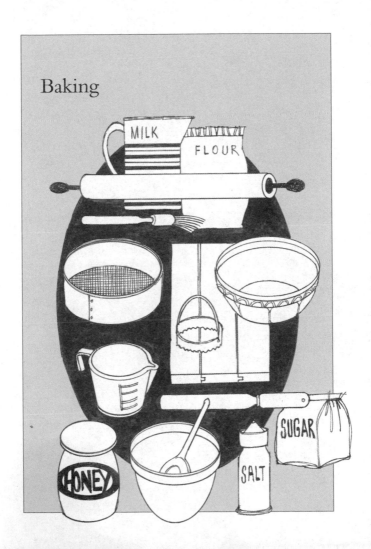

Baking

MILK

FLOUR

HONEY

SALT

SUGAR

Baking with honey

Honey is a versatile ingredient, offering many advantages to both baker and eater. It is sweeter than sugar, so use less when substituting.

Biscuits, sweet and savoury, bake more quickly when made with honey. A lower temperature ensures biscuits bake crisply.

Cakes made with honey colour more quickly. A lower oven temperature will avoid soggy middles and burnt tops.

Honey helps keep cakes, fruit loaves, scones and pancakes moist.

Fat-free sponges baked with honey colour evenly and bake more rapidly. Adding honey to a Swiss roll mixture will help it roll crack-free.

To summarise: Honey helps to cut baking time and temperature, adding colour and flavour to biscuits and cakes.

Honey is hygroscopic, trapping moisture in the crumb, and thus keeps cakes, scones, loaves and tea breads moist for longer. Honey preserves moisture in gluten-free baking. Replace wheat flour by gluten-free self-raising flour in any of the baking recipes here to make a gluten-free option.

Scones and cakes

Tear-and-share sultana honey oat scones

My next door neighbour, Katie, is in her 96th year. Originally from the Hebridean island of Barra, she was brought up on home baking and often talks of a large freshly baked oven scone that was shared by the family. This version takes 5 minutes to prepare.

Makes 8 portions
115g (4oz) self-raising flour
1 level teaspoon baking powder
30g (1oz) oat flakes
30g (1oz) sultanas
30g (1oz) rapeseed or similar cooking oil
30g (1oz) warmed honey
1 large egg
Milk to mix

Turn on the oven at 200°C (fan 180°C), 400°F, Gas 6, and oil a baking tray. Sift the flour into a bowl and add the baking powder, oats and sultanas. Beat the oil with the honey and beaten egg, pour into the bowl and mix, adding sufficient milk to make a soft dough. Turn onto the oiled baking tray and sprinkle the top with oat flakes. Press out gently with the palm of your hand to a round thick scone shape, 5cm (2in) thick. Use a large flat-bladed knife to mark across the circle, in half, then quarters and finally 8 triangles. Bake for 10 to 12 minutes till risen and golden. Cool on the baking tray, loosen the base with a palette knife and lift onto a wire cooling rack when set. Tear apart at the knife-marks to share. Enjoy freshly baked with butter and/or honey.

Honey dropped scones

At a social evening when we were sharing some baking duties, a teacher friend queried whether the dropped scone is a Scots pancake. An interesting discussion followed that lasted all evening, and before we knew it the work was done, so we agreed to re-name dropped scones 'the Dropped Scots Pancake Scones'! Another teacher suggested I add honey and butter to my dropped scones recipe, and so here it is.

Makes 10 to 12 dropped scones
115g (4oz) self-raising flour
1 egg
35g (1 generous oz) pure honey, warmed
90ml (3fl oz) milk
1 level teaspoon baking powder
15g (½oz) melted butter
Vegetable oil

Put a girdle or thick-bottomed frying pan on low to medium heat. Sift the flour into a bowl, add the egg and honey and beat to a soft, thick dropping batter with the milk. A balloon whisk is ideal for this. Stir in the melted butter and baking powder. Test the heat of the girdle with a little flour. If it turns golden, the temperature is correct; if it burns, it is too hot. Oil the heated surface and drop on tablespoons of batter, till bubbles rise and burst on the uncooked surface. Flip over with the flat blade of a palette knife or fish slice, gently tapping the cooked side as you do to release any trapped air and ensure an even bake underneath. Cool on a wire rack, wrapped in a clean tea towel.

The scones freeze well for up to 6 weeks. A gluten-free version can be made, replacing the flour and baking powder with suitable substitutes.

Honey and raspberry Swiss roll

I had the idea of making a Swiss roll with honey. Honey produced a softer sponge, making it easier to roll crack-free! One of the best I have baked.

Makes 1 tin, approximately 23cm (9in) x 30cm (12in)
3 fresh eggs
75g (2½oz) pure honey
45g (1½oz) caster sugar
150g (5½oz) self-raising flour, sifted

For the filling:
3 dessertspoons raspberry jam
3 dessertspoons pure honey

Turn on the oven at 200°C (fan 195°C), 400°F, Gas 6. Oil and line a Swiss roll tin with greaseproof paper. Whisk the eggs with the honey and sugar till thick. Fold in the sifted flour gently, keeping as much air as possible in the mixture. Pour into the prepared tin, smooth with a spatula or palette knife, and tap the base sharply on the work surface to even the mix. Bake in the middle of the oven for 8 to 10 minutes.

Meanwhile, lay a clean damp tea towel flat on the work surface, cover with greaseproof paper and sprinkle evenly with caster sugar. Warm the filling ingredients and mix. The cake is ready when it is golden, firm and springy to gentle pressure. Remove from the oven, loosen the sides with a palette knife and turn, baked side up, onto the sugar-coated paper. Remove the greaseproof paper from the sponge and trim thin edges off the sides with a sharp knife. Spread the surface with the raspberry honey filling.

Take a long knife and mark a line at the right-hand short end of the sponge 2½cm (1in) from the edge. Lifting the greaseproof paper from the right, gently coax the sponge to roll round the filling while warm and soft. Wrap the paper and tea towel round the roll and leave to cool and set on a wire tray. Swiss rolls are notoriously difficult to achieve, but this one rolled like a dream, and stayed moist to the last crumb.

Eat fresh, store in an airtight tin.

Hot toddy Orkney broonie

F. Marian McNeill describes collecting this, her first recipe, in a taped interview with Ernest Marwick lodged in the archives of Kirkwall Library. Each day at school she ate a packed lunch made of what she calls 'plain fare'; a school friend, in contrast, often shared slices of her mother's homemade ginger cake. So good was the cake that Floss, as she was known to her family and friends, asked for the recipe. Thus began her life's work, to collect and preserve our food heritage, which she wrote about in *The Scots Kitchen*, including that original recipe for Orkney Broonie.

Makes 2 x 550g (1¼lb) loaves
350g (12oz) plain flour
115g (4oz) oatmeal
115g (4oz) soft brown sugar
1 teaspoon bicarbonate of soda
1 teaspoon ground ginger
¼ teaspoon chilli powder
¼ teaspoon mixed spice
115g (4oz) butter or margarine
85g (3oz) black treacle
85g (3oz) pure honey
Milk to mix
2 tablespoons very hot water

For the drizzle:
30g (1oz) pure honey, warmed with
1 tablespoon whisky

Turn on the oven at 160°C (fan 140°C), 325°F, Gas 3. Oil and line two loaf tins. Sift the flour, bicarbonate of soda and spices into a bowl and add the oatmeal. Rub in the butter or margarine and stir in the soft brown sugar. Melt the treacle and honey and stir into the mixture with sufficient milk to make a soft dropping consistency, then beat in the hot water. Pour evenly into the two prepared tins and bake in the middle of the oven for 30 to 40 minutes till risen and firm, and the point of a skewer or sharp knife inserted in the middle comes out cleanly. Check the cakes after 30 minutes.

Cool a little in the tins, then pour the drizzle evenly over each and leave to cool completely. Wrap in foil and store in an airtight tin for up to two weeks in a cool place.

Serve spread thickly with butter or on its own. This makes a delicious pudding served warm with fresh cream or custard.

Add 60g (2oz) raisins as a variation.

Fresh fruit, lemon and honey drizzle cake

Bees collect nectar and pollen from the blossoms of spring and early summer. In doing so, they help fertilise fruit-bearing trees and plants, transferring pollen as they forage. The result – a crop of fruit! I like baking fresh fruit with honey in a cake.

175g (6oz) self-raising flour, sifted with
1 level teaspoon each of ground cinnamon and ginger
115g (4oz) Scottish butter
85g (3oz) soft brown sugar
30g (1oz) pure honey, warmed a little
2 eggs, beaten
3 fresh plums, washed, stoned and chopped
1 large eating apple, peeled and cored: chop half and slice half to decorate the top of the cake
1 large handful of fresh blueberries
30g (1oz) dried cranberries

For the drizzle:
30g (1oz) pure honey, warmed with 1 tablespoon fresh lemon juice

---

Oil and line a cake tin 18cm (7in) diameter. Turn on the oven at 160°C (fan 140°C), 325°F, Gas 3. Sift the flour and spices into a bowl. Cream the butter and sugar till light and beat in the honey. Gradually add the egg, alternating with dessertspoons of sifted flour and beat well. Don't worry if the mix curdles.

Sift in the rest of the flour, fold it into the mixture and then stir in the fruits, reserving a few cranberries and the sliced apple to decorate the top. Scrape the cake mix into the prepared tin and smooth the top of the mix with the back of a spoon dipped in hot water. Decorate with a circle of apple slices, arrange cranberries in the middle and round the edges. Bake in the centre of the oven for 45 minutes to 1 hour (check after 45 minutes) till firm and a skewer or sharp knife inserted in the middle of the cake comes out cleanly. Pour the honey lemon drizzle over, leave to soak and cool completely in the tin on a wire rack. Enjoy freshly baked.

Keep in the fridge and eat within four or five days, if it lasts that long!

Drizzles for cakes and loaves

Transform a warm cake, fruit loaf or gingerbread with a honey drizzle.

30g (1oz) pure honey – mix with 1 tablespoon of fresh lemon, orange or lime juice. Cranberry, pomegranate and other sharp fruit juices may be used too.

Raspberry and honey muffins

When I was a child in the 1950s the bakers made muffins, which were pale, yeasted, slightly sweet, soft flat buns. They had an unappetising appearance, being well toasted top and bottom, and somewhat pale round the sides. The range of muffins so popular today bear no resemblance, they are easier to make, and look and taste far more interesting.

Makes 8 muffins
125g (4½oz) self-raising flour
20g (¾oz) caster sugar
30g (1oz) honey
1 large egg
20ml rapeseed oil
Milk to mix
45g (1½oz) fresh or frozen raspberries – broken

To fill the muffins:
1 tablespoon pure honey, warmed

Turn on the oven at 190°C (fan 170°C), 375°F, Gas 5, and arrange 8 muffin cases in a baking tin. Sift the flour into a bowl, add the sugar and stir in the egg beaten with the honey, oil, and sufficient milk to make a soft dropping consistency. Stir in the broken rasps and spoon into the muffin cases. Bake 8 to 12 minutes till risen, golden and set. Cool a little, then, using the handle of a teaspoon, make a hole in the top of each muffin and drop in a teaspoon of honey. Cool on a wire rack.

Enjoy freshly baked and just warm.

Chocolate orange honey cup-cakes

'Cup-cakes' made from a packet mix called 'lemon tops' by Mary Baker were my first baking adventure, aged 7 years old. Add an egg to mix A, beat with a wooden spoon, then deposit into the white paper cases provided. Icing in packet B turned very yellow. My friend Maureen made 'orange tops', the icing for which was equally fluorescent. Since then we have both learned to bake!

Makes 20 to 24 cup-cakes
175g (6oz) self-raising flour
30g (1oz) cocoa
1 teaspoon bicarbonate of soda
125g (4½oz) caster sugar
2 eggs, beaten
150ml (¼ pint) vegetable or sunflower oil
150ml (¼ pint) milk
Grated zest of 1 orange
85g (3oz) pure honey, warmed

To decorate:
Cream crowdie (see page 70)
Chocolate vermicelli
Dark chocolate buttons

Turn on the oven at 160°C (fan 140°C), 325°F, Gas 3, and put 24 cup-cake cases into paté tins. Use a food-mixer or mix by hand. Sift the flour, cocoa powder and bicarbonate of soda into a mixing bowl, add caster sugar and mix. In another bowl beat the eggs, oil and milk, pour into the flour mixture and mix on low speed to combine. Beat on medium speed for 2 to 3 minutes. Add the honey and orange zest and beat for 1 minute.

Pour into the cake cases, only half-filling because the cakes rise, so put less rather than more mix into each. Bake for 10 to 12 minutes till risen and firm. Cool on a wire rack.

Decorate the top with cream crowdie (see page 70), sprinkle with chocolate vermicelli and top each with a dark chocolate button.

Biscuits

Honey oatcakes

I like to use 100% oatmeal to make an oatcake and find
that oatmeal which is medium to fine ground works
well. To prevent the dough sticking, use gluten-free flour
or rice flour to roll out – a tip from a baker friend. It
definitely works.

Makes 18 oatcakes or 2 rounds of 8 triangles
160g (5½oz) fine oatmeal
½ level teaspoon sea salt
Pinch of bicarbonate of soda
15g (½oz) pure honey, warmed a little
20ml (¾oz) sunflower or rapeseed oil
Tepid water

To roll out:
Gluten-free rice flour or oatmeal

Turn on the oven at 180°C (fan 160°C), 350°F, Gas 4. Use
a food-mixer to make mixing easier. Put the oatmeal, sea
salt, and bicarbonate of soda into the mixing bowl and
pour in the warmed honey and oil. Mix on slow speed,
and gradually add tepid water in stages, mixing in
between, till the dough comes together to form a clean,
smooth, pliable ball.

Dust a board with flour or oatmeal and dust the

surface of the dough to prevent sticking. Roll out thinly and cut into round biscuits approx 5cm (2in) in diameter and put onto a non-stick baking tray. Alternatively, divide into two pieces. Roll each into a round and then cut across the diameter into 6 or 8 equal triangles, and use a palette knife or fish slice to lift onto a baking tray.

Bake for 5 to 8 minutes, then turn down the oven to 160°C (fan 140°C), 350°F, Gas 3, to allow the oatcakes to crisp. The triangles will cook in about 10 to 12 minutes and the round biscuits 12 to 15 minutes. Cool on a wire tray and store in an airtight tin.

The triangles are known in Scotland as *farls* and the round of dough from which they are cut, a *bannock*.

Cracked black pepper oatcakes for a change? Add 1 teaspoon of coarse-ground black pepper to the mix. Poppy seeds or sesame seeds can be added too.

Honey mustard oatcakes

The complex flavours of mustard and honey have an
affinity with oats. These go well with strong cheese.

Makes 18 oatcakes 5cm (2in) diameter
100g (3½oz) medium oatmeal
30g (1oz) rolled oats
¼ teaspoon sea salt
Pinch of bicarbonate of soda
15ml (1 tablespoon) vegetable or sunflower oil
20g (¾oz) wholegrain honey mustard or mix mustard with
    honey to taste

To roll out:
Gluten-free rice flour or oatmeal

Turn on the oven at 180°C (fan 160°C), 350°F, Gas 4. Use
a food-mixer if possible to mix the dough. Put the oats,
sea salt, bicarbonate of soda, oil and wholegrain honey
mustard into the bowl and mix on slow speed. Gradually
add tepid water, mixing after each addition, till the dough
becomes a clean, smooth ball. Dust a board with flour or
oatmeal, turn out the dough, dust the top with flour to
prevent sticking, then roll out thinly. Use a 5cm (2in)
cutter to cut out the dough, and bake for 6 to 8 minutes
in the heated oven, then turn down the heat to 160°C
(fan 140°C), 350°F, Gas 4, for a further 5 to 6 minutes till
crisp. Cool on a wire tray and store in an airtight tin.

Heather honey and oat shortbread

This recipe is adapted from one I learned during cookery classes at Elgin Girls Technical College in my secondary school days. I substituted heather honey for sugar and began baking. After trying several variations, all tasters agreed that adding oats enhances the honey flavour.

Makes 21 biscuits 5cm (2in)
60g (2oz) butter, softened
45g (1½oz) pure honey
85g (3oz) self-raising flour
60g (2oz) oatmeal, medium or fine
15g (½oz) cornflour

Turn on the oven at 160°C (fan 140°C), 325°F, Gas 3. Cream the honey and butter till light in colour. Sift the flours into a bowl and add the oatmeal. Stir the flour and oatmeal into the butter/honey mixture at slow speed to mix and form a soft, pliable dough.

Leave for 5 minutes to let the oatmeal swell and thicken the dough, making it easier to roll out. Knead lightly on a floured board and roll out to 5mm (¼in) thick. Cut out with a 5cm (2in) cutter and lay onto non-stick baking trays. Bake for 10 to 12 minutes; watch them carefully, because the biscuits cook quickly.

Dust with caster sugar while warm and cool on a wire rack. Store in an airtight tin.

Topped with cream crowdie (see page 70) and fresh soft fruit, this makes a delicious dessert.

Chewy apple, apricot and honey flapjacks

Honey baked in flapjacks creates a luxurious unctuousness of taste and texture. These treats bake in next to no time, so keep an eye on the oven.

Makes 16 squares baked in a tin 19cm (7½in) square
115g (4oz) butter or margarine
75g (2½oz) pure honey
75g (2½oz) light soft brown sugar
225g (8oz) rolled oats
10g (¼oz) pumpkin seeds
1 eating apple, peeled, cored and grated
30g (1oz) dried chopped apricots

Turn on the oven to heat at 180°C (fan 160°C), 350°F, Gas 4. Oil a suitable baking tin.

Melt the butter or margarine, honey and soft brown sugar together in a pan over a low heat or in the microwave. Stir in the oats, seeds and fruit. Spread the mixture evenly into the tin and bake in the middle of the heated oven for 15 to 20 minutes. Cool in the tin, cutting into squares when still warm. Leave to firm before lifting from the tin with a palette knife. Store in an airtight container.

This is a recipe with endless possibilities: you can add seeds, and other fresh or dried fruits. Remember, fresh fruit will soften the texture.

Fair Maid of Perth biscuits

The Fair Maid of Perth, a novel by Sir Walter Scott, published in 1828, was one of the peaks of his writing career. One chapter describes 'thin soft cakes made of flour and honey according to the family receipt' served to the Fair Maid at breakfast, which inevitably inspired cooks to recreate the recipe for these cakes. Mrs Dalgairns's recipe, originally in her book *The Practice of Cookery*, appears in F. Marian McNeill's *The Scots Kitchen*. However, after two attempts at it, on each of which the Maid would have broken her teeth, I decided to create an alternative. Mine is similar to a Scotch Perkin, and flavoured with citrus and spices just like the original Maid's cakes.

Makes 18 biscuits
115g (4oz) self-raising flour
1 level teaspoon each of ground cinnamon and ginger
Grated zest of 1 lemon
Grated zest of half an orange
45g (1½oz) caster sugar
60g (2oz) pure honey
75g (2½oz) butter
½ teaspoon bicarbonate of soda

Turn on the oven at 160°C (fan 140°C), 325°F, Gas 3. Oil two baking trays. Sift the flour and spices into a bowl, mix in the lemon and orange zest. Melt the sugar, honey and butter together till bubbling. Add the bicarbonate of soda, stirring until it froths. Add the flour mix, and continue to stir till smooth. Drop teaspoons of mix onto the prepared trays, allowing plenty of room to spread. Bake for about 10 to 12 minutes till golden and softly set. Using a palette knife, loosen, lift and lay on a wire cooling tray; do this immediately or the biscuits will stick. They firm as they cool. Store in an airtight tin. These are delicious drizzled with dark chocolate.

Preserves

Old-fashioned lemon honey curd

I remember stirring forever, 'helping' my mother make traditional lemon curd. It was worth the wait. Making lemon curd with honey seemed a natural progression from this and friends have enjoyed the tasting of it. If you like a tangy sharp flavour the recipe below is for you. For a sweeter version add a little more honey.

60g (2oz) butter
60g (2oz) pure honey
2 unwaxed lemons, the juice and finely grated rind
1 whole egg and 1 egg yolk

Put all the ingredients into a heat-resistant bowl. Place the bowl over a simmering pan of water to heat from the steam, but not actually touching the boiling water. Keep stirring till the mixture eventually thickens enough to coat the back of the spoon, and be patient!
Pour into clean jars, seal and label clearly. This makes approximately 150ml (5fl oz) of curd. Store in a cool place for up to 10 days.

Sauces and Relishes

Wholegrain honey mustard sauce

Complements poached salmon, baked trout or roast pheasant. Excellent served with a fish starter.

Serves 4
25g (scant 1oz) wholegrain honey mustard
1 teaspoon heather honey
60g (2oz) mayonnaise
Squeeze of fresh lemon juice.

Mix all together and it is ready to serve.

Honey garlic sauce

This sauce is a revelation, as a dip, with smoked and cured meats, and cheeses. It also makes a good marinade.

15g (½oz) heather honey
1 tablespoon soy sauce
1 tablespoon cider vinegar
1 large clove fresh garlic, crushed
1 piece of root ginger, approximately 1 inch, peeled and grated

Mix all together, infuse for 10 minutes, and the sauce is ready to serve.

Honey vinaigrette

Adds flavour and health to salads and vegetables.

Basic recipe:
1 tablespoon apple cider vinegar
1 tablespoon pure honey, add more to taste if liked
3 tablespoons extra virgin olive oil or Scottish rapeseed oil
Freshly ground black pepper
Sea salt

Put all the ingredients into a jar, screw on the lid and
shake to make.

Suggested additions: citrus juices, herbs, flavoured oils,
yoghurt.

Honey marinade

Honey is a natural marinade. Rub over meat, poultry,
game or oily fish, cover and leave at least 1 hour before
cooking, then bake, grill, barbecue or roast.

To finish a roast, rub with extra honey and crisp for
30 minutes in a hot oven at the end of cooking.

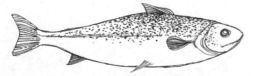

Honey mayonnaise

Honey is a natural emulsifier, and so helpful in all mayonnaise-style sauces. A simple honey mayonnaise takes little time and is worth the effort.

Makes approximately 200ml (7fl oz)
150ml (¼ pint) rapeseed oil
1 tablespoon apple cider vinegar
1 tablespoon fresh lemon juice
1 level teaspoon sea salt
1 level teaspoon mustard powder
Freshly ground black pepper
15g (½oz) pure honey
Yolk of a large fresh egg

Lay a damp cloth under the bowl to prevent it moving. Pour the oil, vinegar and lemon juice into separate jugs. Put the salt, mustard, pepper, honey and egg yolk into the bowl and whisk together. Whisking continuously, slowly, a little at a time, pour the oil into the mix and then the vinegar and lemon juice, whisking vigorously between each addition. Taste and adjust the seasoning. Pour into a sealed container and store in the fridge for up to five days.

Christmas recipes

A honey-enriched traditional fruit cake

Christmas would not be the same without the aroma of a slowly baking fruit cake pervading the house. Each year I enjoy creating a new recipe, baked as a gift for friends. This year, I discovered that adding honey to a fruit cake keeps it moist and full of flavour.

Makes 1 round cake for a 20cm (8in) tin

Fruit:
140g (5oz) sultanas
140g (5oz) raisins
85g (3oz) chopped dried apricots
60g (2oz) dried cranberries
50g (1¼oz) mixed peel

Cake:
175g (6oz) fresh unsalted butter
140g (5oz) soft brown sugar
60g (2oz) pure honey, warmed slightly to soften
175g (6oz) self-raising flour
1 level teaspoon ground cinnamon
1 level teaspoon mixed spice
Pinch of nutmeg
1 level teaspoon baking powder
3 large fresh eggs, beaten
Grated zest and juice of 1 large orange

Drizzle:
1 dessertspoon of warmed honey mixed with
2 tablespoons fresh orange juice and
1 tablespoon whisky

Turn on the oven at 160°C (fan 140°C), 325°F, Gas 3. Oil and line the cake tin with greaseproof paper. Weigh the fruits and put them into a bowl. Sift the flour, spices and baking powder into a bowl. Beat the soft brown sugar and butter together till light and stir in the softened honey. Gradually beat in the eggs, alternating with a spoon of sifted flour to prevent the mixture curdling. Fold in the rest of the flour, with 2 tablespoons of fresh orange juice and orange zest, and lastly stir in the fruit till evenly mixed. Spoon carefully into the prepared tin, making sure that the mix is even. Wet a clean hand and use the palm to flatten and smooth the cake, especially in the middle to help prevent the cake rising to a peak in baking. Put into the oven.

After 40 minutes, turn down the heat to 130°C (fan 110°C), 250°F, Gas 1. Bake a further 15 to 20 minutes. Test the middle of the cake by gently inserting a skewer or sharp knife. If it comes out cleanly and the cake feels firm and springy to gentle pressure, it is ready. If not, bake a further 5 to 10 minutes and test again. Remove from the oven, and while still warm, spoon the drizzle over and cool in the tin on a wire rack overnight. Wrap in foil and keep in a cool place for up to one week to allow the cake to mature. Marzipan and ice as required.

Honey and walnut mincemeat tarts

Honey mincemeat

Honey in mincemeat instead of sugar makes it moist and juicy. Vary the fruit, including fresh and dried according to taste.

115g (4oz) raisins
115g (4oz) sultanas
115g (4oz) chopped apricots
115g (4oz) chopped dried figs
60g (2oz) chopped mixed peel
3 apples, peeled, cored and grated
Grated rind and juice of one lemon
2 tablespoons tangy orange marmalade
60g (2oz) vegetarian suet (if liked)
100g (3½oz) pure honey
1 teaspoon ground cinnamon
½ teaspoon mixed spice
¼ teaspoon ground nutmeg
150ml (¼ pint) brandy, whisky or sherry

Put all the ingredients into a bowl and mix together. Store in an airtight container in the fridge and keep for two or three days before use to allow the flavour to develop.

Walnut and honey pastry

Ground walnuts add crunch and a hint of honey gives subtle sweetness.

Makes enough pastry for 18 to 24 tarts
115g (4oz) butter or margarine
225g (8oz) plain flour
30g (1oz) ground walnuts
15g (½oz) pure honey, warmed a little to soften
Cold water to mix

Rub the butter or margarine into the flour till it resembles fine breadcrumbs, then stir in the walnuts and honey along with sufficient water to make a pliable clean dough. Leave it to rest for 10 minutes.

To finish the tarts:
1 egg, beaten
Caster sugar

Turn on the oven at 200°C (fan 180°C), 400°F, Gas 6. Oil two patty-tin trays. Roll the pastry on a floured board to 3mm (⅛in) thick, cut into rounds a little bigger than the rounds of the patty tins. Line the tins with the pasty, then add mincemeat to fill them two-thirds deep. Cut slightly smaller rounds of pastry for the tops, damp the edges, place on top of the mincemeat, and press the pastry edges together. Make two slits on top of each pie with the tip of a sharp knife. Brush with beaten egg. Put on baking trays to catch any drips while baking. Bake for 15 to 20 minutes till golden. Dust with caster sugar when warm, and cool on a wire track. The pies can be made in advance and cooked from frozen; this takes 5 minutes longer.

As a variation, try topping the mincemeat with grated marzipan instead of pastry.

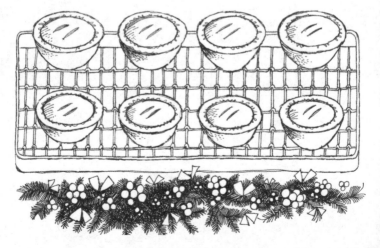

Beverages

Some up-to-date, quick drinks ideas
for your jar of pure honey.

Smoothies

Smoothies are a great way to eat 'five a day' or more.

Per serving, allow 140g (5oz) berries, choosing from soft fruits such as blueberries, raspberries, strawberries, loganberries, plus a small banana or apple, and peaches and mango in season.

Add a generous teaspoon of pure honey. Blitz till smooth with approximately 150ml (¼ pint) apple or orange juice, or use dairy or any other of the alternative milks now available. Softly frozen chunks of skinned banana blitz to a cool thick creamy smoothness. Lightly frozen soft fruits help make a deliciously cold smoothie on a hot summer day.

Blenshaw

Blenshaw is a corruption of the French words 'blanche eau' which mean 'white water'. A friend adds a tot of brandy or whisky to her evening mug of Blenshaw to help her sleep.

Serves 1
1 teaspoon oatmeal
1 teaspoon pure honey
2 tablespoons creamy milk
Boiling water
A little grated nutmeg (optional)
A tot of brandy (optional)

Mix the oatmeal and honey with the milk in a large mug and stir till smooth. Keep stirring while you add boiling water to fill the mug, and add a grating of nutmeg and/or brandy if liked. Drink warm.

Mummy Clerk's old-fashioned lemonade

Mummy Clerk, as we all knew her, lived next door. She was a great cook, and we as children loved going to visit. In the summer she made lemonade and kindly gave the recipe to my mother. This version is made with pure honey instead of sugar.

Makes 1.4 litres (2½ pints) of lemonade
1.4 litres (2½ pints) water
Zest and juice of 2 oranges
Zest and juice of 2 lemons
125g (4½oz) pure honey

Bring the water to the boil and add the fruit zests and juices. Turn off the heat, and stir in the honey while warm. Cover and leave in a cool place overnight to allow the flavour to develop. Strain and bottle. Chill in the fridge, dilute with still or sparkling water.

Stokos

This traditional drink was made at harvest time to refresh the men, women and children as they worked gathering grain. It is sometimes called 'Harvest Drink'.

Makes 1 litre (1¾ pints)
30g (1oz) oatmeal
Juice of 1 lemon
30g (1oz) pure honey
1 litre (1¾ pints) boiling water

Put the oatmeal, lemon juice and honey into a deep bowl and mix together with a little warm water. Pour over the boiling water, stirring all the time to mix. Cover and leave to cool overnight. Strain into a jug, chill and serve. Occasionally a piece of root ginger was added to the hot mix. The drink was said to be strengthening.

Craig's Atholl brose

My school friend Craig moved 20 years ago to the Limousin area of France, where he has become part of the community. For special occasions he makes his own version of Atholl brose which, as he puts it, 'goes down well with locals hereabouts'. This is Craig's recipe.

1.5 litre (2¾ pints) bottle of still spring water
150g (5½oz) porridge oats or oatmeal
85g (3oz) pure honey
1 bottle of reasonably priced whisky, a blend will be fine

'Allow one week to make this. Take the bottle of water and remove half a litre (16 fl oz), add the porridge oats to the bottle (cannot buy oatmeal here), leave for about 1 week. Shake every time you remember, think about it, or walk by the bottle. On the day of the event, sieve the soggy oats out but retain the liquid and return to the bottle with 85g (3oz) honey and top up the bottle with whisky. Serve at table as a drink remembering to keep the bottle shaken to mix the ingredients.

You may use that in a chapter of your book, at no extra charge!'

Bonne santé, Monsieur Craig!

Yuletide hot ale with honey and spices

This recipe works just as well with cider or red wine. A non-alcoholic version is easily made, substituting apple and red grape juice for the ale, to serve those not wishing to indulge!

Makes 1.2 litres (2 pints)

4 small firm eating apples, peeled, cored and quartered
1 tablespoon pure honey
1 tablespoon water
1.2 litres (2 pints) light ale
1 tablespoon pure honey
1 cinnamon stick
1 piece of root ginger, about 5cm (2in), peeled and cut into thick slices
Juice of 1 orange and a handful of shredded rind
Grating of nutmeg or a generous pinch of ground nutmeg

Put the apple quarters into a pan, add 1 tablespoon of honey and 1 tablespoon of water, bring to the boil, then reduce the heat to simmer, cover the pan and cook till tender but not coloured. Turn off the heat. Take a large pan, add the ale, 1 tablespoon of honey, cinnamon stick, ginger, orange juice and rind, then heat very slowly till just below a simmering boil. Keep at this heat for 10 to 15 minutes to infuse the flavours. Do not allow the pan to boil. Turn off the heat and pour into a punch bowl, add the cooked apples and their juices. Ladle while hot into warm mugs. This is definitely a drink for a cold frosty night.

Hot toddy

'Toddy is excellent both as a cure for a cold and as an elixir of life. It requires careful preparation.' – F. Marian McNeill, *The Scots Cellar*.

Serves 1
2 teaspoons pure honey
Whisky
Boiling water

Heat a glass tumbler by rinsing with boiling water. Add the honey and 1 tablespoon of boiling water to dissolve, add 90 ml (3fl oz) of whisky and stir, add 150ml of boiling water and then 90ml (3fl oz) more whisky (if liked). Stir again. Drink hot.

'Sip the toddy with slow loving care.' – F. Marian McNeill, *The Scots Cellar*.